AF360528

'8-93-5741

)78-93-933

man n

1e end

ent.

out th

e an e

ıs with

rce and

....

d Activ

K, as r

drive a

1

rst sight

osest an

ɔ that.

ıner bu

enquir

out a bl

ame a:

vas lost

membe
ery fas

an to v

ly, so w

ill   call

ill be w

d I was

er I wa

unkno

ion con

ars....lt

ιy I felt

our SA

.

I canr

ɔu and

et, con

.GA

.ot wan
...SHRI

that n

can n

1

1atever

....this s

?...Naał

st me a
e with

to my
she wa

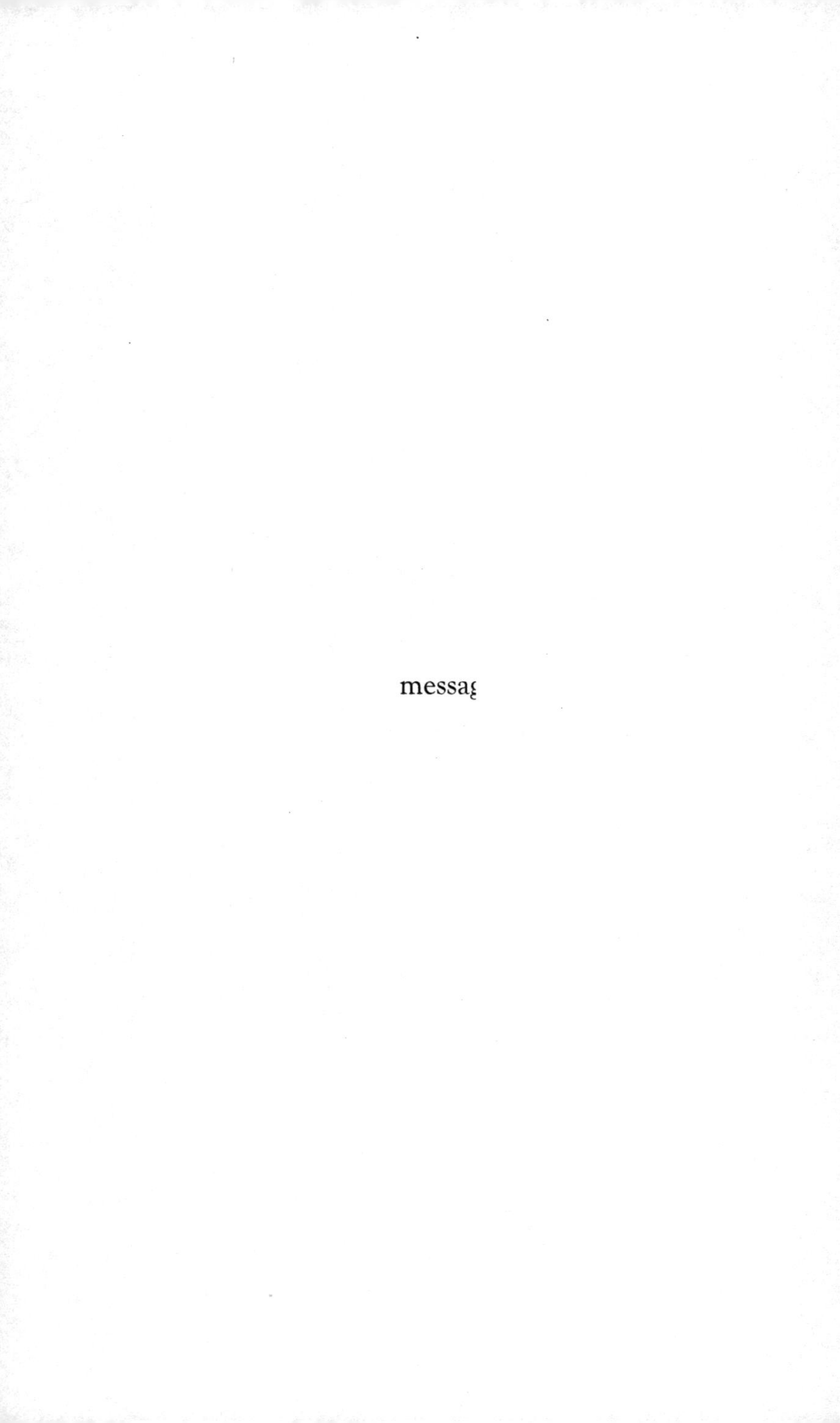

messag

veryone

der th

lf, mak

own wa

itler.....
v love

d look :

.s fair c

was A

ı hand]

ged. Ye
unliki

. you d
. I told

ffice. V
e room

the pla
'v dear'

packing

to my l

son she

; wonde

ow and

as I w

Jot ove
and a

ictures.

re for l

d had 1

ı a pers

the raiı

at good

was ac

1e by n
1re the (

r, be it
d with

d I get
aid o g

on his
ou ask

een as]
pletely 1

red as
amazin

l me. It
served

tried s
st in h

arrive

ıg for h

the thi
All the

very dif

u UN

gs into

: for n

;em I h
now ab

hieved

to stan

to get

want y

.e can t
forever.

apa ke
bulan

ıar ham

www.ingramcontent.com/pod-product-compliance
Lightning Source LLC
LaVergne TN
LVHW091216180726
843490LV00007B/2779